Sweet Treats

WITH A SIDE SERVING OF SCIENCE

by M.M. Eboch

raintree
a Capstone company — publishers for children

Raintree is an imprint of Capstone Global Library Limited, a company incorporated in England and Wales having its registered office at 264 Banbury Road, Oxford, OX2 7DY – Registered company number: 6695582

www.raintree.co.uk
myorders@raintree.co.uk

Edited by Abby Colich
Designed by Juliette Peters
Original illustrations © Capstone Global Library Limited 2019
Picture research by Tracy Cummins
Photo and Food Stylist: Sarah Schuette; images by Capstone Studio (Karon Dubke)
Production by Laura Manthe
Originated by Capstone Global Library Ltd
Printed and bound in India

ISBN 978 1 4747 5727 0 (paperback)
22 21 20 19 18
10 9 8 7 6 5 4 3 2 1

British Library Cataloguing in Publication Data
A full catalogue record for this book is available from the British Library.

Acknowledgements
We would like to thank the following for permission to reproduce photographs:
Capstone Studio: Karon Dubke.

Contents

Let's get cooking!

Imagine having your very own science lab. It has plenty of space. It has all of the materials you need for your experiments. It has tools to measure those materials. It even has a source of heat. Basically, it's a kitchen!

Cooking is like doing science experiments. Ingredients are mixed together and heated. Reactions occur. You don't need to know how the science works, but it can be helpful to know why some cookies are soft and others crispy, and why lollipops are hard. Understanding what happens, and why, can help you if something goes wrong.

KITCHEN SAFETY

Safety should be your top priority in the kitchen. Make sure an adult can help you before beginning any recipe. Follow these safety tips:

- Wash your hands before beginning any recipe. Wash them again after touching raw ingredients such as eggs.

- Be careful when touching hot pans, utensils or food. Use oven gloves when transferring hot items or ask an adult to do this for you.

- Sweet mixtures may bubble and splatter. Don't let the hot mixture touch your skin. It can cause burns. Ask an adult to help you.

- Don't taste uncooked dough if it contains eggs. Raw eggs may make you ill.

- Use caution when using a sharp knife.

NOW HEAD TO YOUR KITCHEN SCIENCE LAB FOR SOME TASTY EXPERIMENTS!

THE KEY TO GREAT CUPCAKES

All the cupcake recipes in this book require a few of the same steps. Follow these steps for great cupcakes every time!

• Put a rack in the middle of the oven. Then turn on your oven and let it fully preheat.

• When you see "prepare your tin", put cupcake cases in the cupcake tin. If you don't have cases, lightly grease the tin with some butter or cooking oil. This will stop the cupcakes sticking.

• Fill each cupcake case three-quarters full, unless otherwise noted. Do not overfill. If you have batter left over, make a second partial batch.

• Set a timer for the lowest time mentioned in the recipe. When the timer dings, insert a toothpick or cake tester into a cupcake. The tester should come out clean or with only a few moist crumbs attached.

• After cupcakes have finished baking, place the tin on a rack and cool for 5 to 10 minutes. Then remove from the tin and allow to cool completely before icing. Icing can lose its fluffiness over time. Ice the cupcakes just before serving them.

• Store cupcakes in the fridge for up to four days. Let them come to room temperature before serving. For longer storage, freeze the cupcakes in an airtight container for up to three months.

CONVERSION CHART

Here's a handy conversion guide if your scales use imperial measurements or you have a gas cooker.

WEIGHT

½ ounce = 10 grams
¾ ounce = 20 grams
1 ounce = 25 grams

TEMPERATURE

140°C = Gas mark 1
150°C = Gas mark 2
170°C = Gas mark 3
180°C = Gas mark 4
190°C = Gas mark 5
200°C = Gas mark 6
220°C = Gas mark 7

TIP ....

For more information about the techniques used in this book, turn to page 30 before you begin.

Chocolate Cherry Cupcakes

Mmm. Chocolate and cherries are so good together! This treat starts with a rich chocolate cupcake, but it doesn't stop there. A spoonful of cherry pie filling goes in the centre of each. Fluffy cherry icing tops it off. If you want even more cherry flavour, use cherry extract instead of vanilla in both the cupcake and the icing. Your taste-testers will be cheering for cherry!

INGREDIENTS

200 g plain flour
¼ teaspoon bicarbonate of soda
2 teaspoons baking powder
115 g unsweetened cocoa
    powder
¼ teaspoon salt
45 g butter, softened
340 g caster sugar
2 eggs
1 teaspoon vanilla extract or
    cherry extract
240 ml milk
1 tin of red cherry pie filling

ICING

225 g salted butter, softened
750 g icing sugar
1 teaspoon vanilla extract or
    cherry extract
2 to 3 drops red food colouring
12 cherries

EQUIPMENT

12-cup cupcake tin and cases
measuring spoons
mixing bowls
electric mixer
weighing scales
melon baller or spoon
knife

1 Preheat the oven to 180°C. Prepare your cupcake tin.

2 In a medium bowl, mix the flour, bicarbonate of soda, baking powder, cocoa powder and salt. Set aside.

3 In a large bowl, combine the butter and caster sugar. Blend with the electric mixer until light and fluffy.

4 Add the eggs to the butter mixture one at a time, mixing after each one is added. Blend in the vanilla or cherry extract.

5 Add half of the flour mixture to the butter mixture and blend well. Blend in the milk. Add the remaining flour mixture and blend well.

6 Divide the batter into the cupcake cases, filling each about three-quarters full. Bake for 15 to 17 minutes. Allow to cool completely.

7 Make the icing. Place the butter in a large bowl. Beat with an electric mixer until fluffy. Blend in the icing sugar, vanilla or cherry extract and food colouring. Beat until creamy.

8 Using a melon baller or spoon, scoop a small hole into the top of each cupcake. Drop a spoonful of cherry pie filling into each hole. Replace scooped out part of the cupcake over the filling.

9 Spread or pipe the icing on the cooled cupcakes. Top each cupcake with a cherry.

cookie dough cupcakes

What could be better than freshly-baked chocolate chip cookies? How about putting one inside a cupcake! These chocolate chip cupcakes have a ball of chocolate chip cookie dough in the centre. As they bake, heat surrounds the outside of the cupcakes first, then works its way towards the centre. The cookie dough ball bakes less than the outer cupcake, leaving it doughy. But it is heated enough to kill any bacteria, making it safe to eat.

INGREDIENTS	ICING	EQUIPMENT
1 packet of cookie dough	90 g soft brown sugar	12-cup cupcake tin and cases
300 g plain flour	50 g icing sugar	measuring spoons
2 teaspoons baking powder	115 g butter	weighing scales
½ teaspoon salt	1 teaspoon vanilla extract	mixing bowls
115 g butter, softened	150 g plain flour	whisk
170 g caster sugar	½ teaspoon salt	electric mixer
2 eggs	2 to 6 tablespoons milk, as	toothpick or cake tester
1 teaspoon vanilla extract	needed	
240 ml milk	150 g chocolate chips	
150 g chocolate chips		

1 Roll a tablespoon of cookie dough into a ball. Repeat until you have 12 balls. Chill them in the fridge while you continue to work.

2 Preheat the oven to 190°C. Prepare your cupcake tin.

3 In a medium bowl, whisk together the flour, baking powder and salt. Set aside.

4 In a large bowl, cream the butter and caster sugar until it is light and fluffy. Add the eggs one at a time, mixing after each one is added. Blend in the vanilla extract.

5 Continue mixing slowly as you add half of the dry mixture. Keep mixing as you add the milk. Blend in the remaining flour mixture. Stir in the chocolate chips.

6 Remove cookie dough balls from the fridge. Place one into each cupcake case. Spoon the cupcake batter over each ball of dough, filling each case about three-quarters full.

7 Bake for 18 to 20 minutes. A toothpick inserted into the edge of the cupcakes should come out clean. The cookie dough balls may still be sticky. Cool completely.

8 To make the icing, place the brown sugar, icing sugar, butter and vanilla extract in a mixing bowl. Mix with an electric mixer on low until combined and creamy. Add the flour and salt. Mix on medium speed until blended and creamy. Slowly add milk until the icing is a good thickness for spreading. Use a spoon to stir in the chocolate chips.

9 Spread or pipe the icing on the cooled cupcakes.

CHEMICALS RISE UP

Do you want chemicals in your cupcakes? The idea may sound scary, but you do! Chemical leaveners are ingredients that cause a chemical reaction in cooking and baking. Bicarbonate of soda and baking powder are the most common chemical leaveners. When these ingredients are mixed into a batter, they start releasing carbon dioxide. This is the gas that creates bubbles of air inside the batter. As the cupcakes heat in the oven, the air bubbles continue to expand. These bubbles are like little balloons that make the baked item rise. As the item bakes, the dough or batter solidifies around the bubbles. The air pockets remain after the gas escapes.

Rainbow cupcakes

Would you like to taste a rainbow? This recipe starts with white chocolate cupcakes. Food colouring is added, and the batter is layered to create a colourful interior. The icing is also tinted in rainbow colours. The results are fun to serve at parties. Or provide the baked cupcake, along with icing, in bags to your party guests. Then let your friends decorate their own cupcakes!

INGREDIENTS

115 g butter
170 g caster sugar
2 eggs
150 g white chocolate chips
1 teaspoon vanilla extract
265 g plain flour
1 teaspoon baking powder
¼ teaspoon salt
240 ml milk
red, orange, yellow, green and
  blue food colouring

ICING

600 g icing sugar
225 g butter, softened
1 teaspoon vanilla extract
2 to 3 tablespoons milk
red, orange, yellow, green and
  blue food colouring

EQUIPMENT

12-cup cupcake tin and cases
measuring and mixing spoons
weighing scales
mixing bowls
microwave-safe bowl
microwave
electric mixer
10 small bowls
small (sandwich size) plastic
  food bags

1 Preheat the oven to 170°C. Prepare your cupcake tin.

2 Place the butter and caster sugar in a mixing bowl. Blend with an electric mixer on medium until the mixture is fluffy. Add the eggs one at a time, mixing until just combined.

3 Place the white chocolate chips in the microwave in a microwave-safe bowl. Melt for 30 seconds. Stir well. If necessary, heat for another 10 seconds and check again.

4 Pour the melted chips into the batter. Add the vanilla extract. Mix for about 1 minute.

5 In a separate bowl, combine the flour, baking powder and salt. Add to the wet ingredients and combine. Add half the milk and combine. Repeat for the remaining dry ingredients and milk.

6 Divide the batter into five bowls. They should be roughly equal, but you don't need to measure. Add 2 to 3 drops of one colour of food colouring to each bowl. Mix each with a clean spoon.

7 Evenly divide the red batter among the cupcake cases. Repeat with the remaining colours. To make a rainbow, follow this order: red, orange, yellow, green, blue. When finished, each cupcake case should be about three-quarters full.

8 Bake for 18 to 20 minutes. Allow to cool.

9 Meanwhile, make the icing. In a clean mixing bowl, combine the icing sugar and butter. Beat on low speed until blended. Add the vanilla extract and 2 tablespoons of milk. Mix until smooth. If necessary, add the extra milk, a dribble at a time, until the icing is spreadable.

10 Divide the icing into five bowls. Add 2 to 3 drops of one colour of food colouring to each bowl and mix well. Place each colour of icing in a separate plastic bag. Seal each bag and snip off one lower corner.

11 Top the cooled cupcakes with the icing. Twist the top of the bag to squeeze icing out of the hole. Make a rainbow on top of each cupcake.

Microwave oat cookie

Baking cookies can be a lot of fun, but sometimes you want a treat now. These cookies take only 5 minutes to make! They are perfect for when you want a sweet treat but don't have a lot of time. Microwave cookies are best eaten straight away. Otherwise they can quickly go hard or soggy. This recipe makes a single serving. No waiting and no leftovers!

INGREDIENTS

40 g quick-cooking oats
2 teaspoons flour
2 teaspoons brown sugar
¼ teaspoon baking powder
dash of cinnamon
2 tablespoons apple sauce

¼ teaspoon vanilla extract
1 tablespoon raisins

EQUIPMENT

mixing bowl
microwave-safe plate
cooking spray
measuring and mixing spoons
weighing scales
microwave

1 In a small bowl, mix the oats, flour, brown sugar, baking powder and cinnamon.

2 Stir in the apple sauce and vanilla extract and mix. Stir in the raisins.

3 Spray a microwave-safe plate with cooking spray or lightly grease with butter. Scoop the dough onto the plate. Press it into a cookie shape.

4 Microwave the cookie on high for 60 seconds. Keep in microwave for 1 minute. If the cookie still looks doughy, reheat for an additional 10 seconds. Repeat if needed.

TIP....................

Cooking times can vary between microwaves. You may need to experiment to find the right cooking time for this recipe.

Kitchen Science

MICROWAVE COOKING

A microwave oven uses electromagnetic radiation. These are waves of electrical and magnetic energy that move through space. In other words, a microwave creates energy waves. These waves penetrate food. They cause water molecules in the food to vibrate. The friction caused by the vibration heats the food. Many foods cook more quickly in a microwave than in an ordinary oven. But the air in a microwave is not heated. That means microwaves can't brown the surface of most foods. Because browning is important in most baking, ordinary oven baking is usually the preferred method.

Two-for-one cookie dough brownies

Dense, chewy chocolate brownies are so delicious, but chocolate chip cookies are amazing too. How do you choose which to make? With this recipe, you don't need to! A rich brownie layer is topped with raw chocolate chip cookie dough. The cookie dough layer does not contain eggs, so it's safe to eat.

INGREDIENTS	COOKIE DOUGH LAYER	EQUIPMENT
4 large eggs	115 g butter	baking tray, 20 x 30 cm
190 g unsweetened cocoa powder	55 g caster sugar	mixing bowls
1 teaspoon salt	90 g soft brown sugar	measuring and mixing spoons
1 teaspoon baking powder	3 tablespoons milk	electric mixer
1 tablespoon vanilla extract	1 teaspoon vanilla extract	microwave-safe bowl
225 g butter	150 g plain flour	toothpick or cake tester
500 g caster sugar	150 g chocolate chips	wire cooling rack
225 g flour		weighing scales

1 Preheat oven to 180°C. Grease the baking tray.

2 In a mixing bowl, use the electric mixer to lightly beat the eggs. Add the cocoa, salt, baking powder and vanilla extract. Beat at medium speed for about 1 minute, until smooth.

3 In a medium microwave-safe bowl, melt the butter. Add the caster sugar and stir to combine.

4 Add the butter and sugar mixture to the other ingredients and stir to combine. Fold in the flour.

5 Pour the batter into the baking tray. Bake for around 30 minutes. Use a toothpick or cake tester inserted into the centre to test the brownie is cooked. It should come out clean or with only a few moist crumbs clinging to it. Place the tray on a cooling rack.

6 Make the cookie dough layer. Cream the butter and both sugars in a mixing bowl. Stir in the milk and vanilla extract. Fold in the flour. Stir in the chocolate chips.

7 Drop spoonfuls of cookie dough over the cooled brownies. Spread the cookie dough layer evenly. Cut the brownies into squares or bars and store them in the fridge in an airtight container.

Kitchen Science

SWEET AND SOFT

White sugar and brown sugar are similar. They both come from sugar cane or sugar beets. The two sugars act quite differently in baking, though. All sugar is hygroscopic, meaning it absorbs moisture from the air. Brown sugar is more hygroscopic than white sugar. Brown sugar naturally contains 10 times as much moisture as white sugar. This extra moisture means cookies made with brown sugar are softer. Dark brown sugar has more moisture than light brown sugar. Therefore, using dark brown sugar will result in the softest cookies. Using only white sugar will give crisper cookies. In humid climates, the air holds a lot of moisture. Cookies become softer over time, as they absorb moisture from the air.

Lemon-iced sour cream cookies

If you like cake, you'll love these sour cream cookies. They are soft and tender with a cakey texture that melts in your mouth. A tangy lemon flavour balances out this delicate cookie. Lemon icing adds even more citrus zing, while edible glitter gives it a sparkle.

INGREDIENTS	ICING	EQUIPMENT
55 g butter	55 g butter	baking trays
225 g caster sugar	225 g icing sugar	baking parchment
2 large eggs	1 tablespoon lemon juice	weighing scales
80 ml sour cream	(from 1 lemon)	mixing bowls
1 tablespoon lemon zest	2 to 3 drops yellow food	measuring and mixing spoons
(from 2 lemons)	colouring, optional	electric mixer
1 tablespoon lemon juice	edible glitter or cake sprinkles	wire cooling rack
(from 1 lemon)		butter knife
300 g plain flour		
¼ teaspoon bicarbonate of soda		
2 teaspoons baking powder		

1 Preheat the oven to 180°C. Line the baking trays with baking parchment.

2 Place the butter and caster sugar in a large bowl. Beat with the electric mixer until smooth, for about 3 minutes.

3 Add the eggs, sour cream, lemon zest and lemon juice. Mix until well blended.

4 In a separate bowl, mix the flour, bicarbonate of soda and baking powder. Add to the butter mixture and stir until just combined. The dough will be sticky and soft, like a thick cake batter.

5 Drop the dough in heaped spoonfuls onto the baking trays, at least 5 cm apart. Bake for 10 to 12 minutes, until the centres are firm and the edges are golden.

6 Allow cookies to rest on the tray for 5 minutes, then transfer to a rack to cool.

7 Make the icing. Beat the butter and icing sugar until smooth. Add 1 tablespoon lemon juice and the food colouring, and mix well. If needed, add a little water to make a spreadable, smooth and thick icing.

8 Ice the cookies when they are completely cooled. Swirl the icing onto the cookies with a butter knife. Sprinkle with edible glitter or cake sprinkles. Store cookies in an airtight container.

cinnamon heart lollipops

Show some love with heart-shaped lollipops! These pretty, tasty treats are great for parties or any time. Use another shape if you don't have heart moulds. You'll cook these sweets at a high temperature so they harden properly.

INGREDIENTS

450 g granulated sugar
½ teaspoon cream of tartar
175 g liquid glucose
120 ml cherry juice
dash of ground cinnamon
coloured sugar sprinkles or
    sparkling sugar

EQUIPMENT

heart-shaped lollipop moulds
cooking spray
kitchen roll
lollipop sticks
weighing scales
measuring and mixing spoons
medium saucepan
metal (heatproof) spoon
jam thermometer
cling film

1 Spray the lollipop moulds lightly with cooking spray. Gently wipe out the moulds with a piece of kitchen roll, leaving only a very thin layer of the spray. Place the lollipop sticks in the moulds.

2 In a medium saucepan, combine the sugar, cream of tartar, liquid glucose and cherry juice over medium-high heat. Stir well. Bring to a boil. Stir regularly to dissolve the sugar.

3 Attach the jam thermometer to the saucepan. Without stirring, cook until the temperature reaches 150°C, about 20 minutes.

4 Remove the mixture from the heat. Stir in the cinnamon. Allow the bubbles to break up and disappear.

5 Use a metal spoon to carefully scoop up a heaped spoonful of the mixture. Gently spoon the mixture into a lollipop mould. Make sure the end of the lollipop stick is entirely covered.

6 Quickly repeat step 5 until all the mixture has been used. If the syrup becomes too thick, warm it over low heat.

7 Sprinkle coloured or sparkling sugar over the lollipops. Allow the lollipops to cool.

8 Remove the lollipops from the moulds. Wrap individually in cling film. Store them in an airtight container at room temperature.

Kitchen Science

HEAT IS ENERGY

Everything is made up of molecules. Molecules are tiny particles that are too small to see. They are constantly vibrating, although we can't see or feel this. Heat is a form of energy that moves between molecules. When you put a pan of water on the hob and turn on the heat, the heat from the hob transfers to the molecules in the pan. Then it transfers to the molecules in the water. As the water heats, its molecules vibrate faster. Molecules can combine in different ways too. For example, sugar and water molecules bind together. Some of the water evaporates, turning into steam. All this is caused by the addition of heat. In scientific terms, cooking is just transferring energy by adding heat.

Gummy Stars

Gummy sweets are fun to make and to eat! These colourful stars are great to snack on or to share with friends. The orange gummies are tart while the grape gummies are sweet. Once you've mastered this recipe, you can experiment with different juices and colours.

1 Place 1½ leaves of gelatin in a bowl of cold water. Allow to soften for about 5 minutes.

2 In a medium saucepan, combine the softened gelatin with the grape juice and 85 g liquid glucose or honey. Cook over medium heat until the gelatin dissolves.

3 Add several drops of purple food colouring. Carefully spoon the hot mixture into the moulds. The gummy candy shrinks as it cools, so fill the moulds as full as possible.

4 Refrigerate the sweets for 1 hour, until firm. Remove from the moulds, and store in an airtight container.

5 Repeat steps 1 to 4 using the orange juice and orange food colouring for the orange gummy sweets.

TIP······················

If a recipe says that an ingredient is separated, that means the total amount listed will not be used all at once. Read through the recipe to see how much is needed at each stage.

Kitchen Science

HEAT AND TEMPERATURE

Temperature is a way of measuring energy. However, two things can have different amounts of energy at the same temperature. It depends on the number of molecules. Water has more molecules than air. A pan of water contains more molecules than the same pan full of air. With more molecules, the pan of water has more energy than the pan of air. This means water heated to 121 degrees Celsius (°C) or 250 degrees Fahrenheit (°F) feels hotter than air heated to 121°C (250°F). You can quickly place a pan into an oven heated to 121°C without being hurt. If you stick your hand into water heated to 121°C, you would get a severe burn! (**Don't try this!**) The water has more energy, which would transfer into your hand. That energy, in the form of heat, causes a burn.

Honeycomb treats

What's all the buzz about? Honeycomb is as tasty as it is fun! The bicarbonate of soda makes bubbles that are trapped inside this sweet treat. It leaves a design that looks like a bee's honeycomb. Real honeycombs are actually a collection of hexagon-shaped cells. Bees make them with wax. They use them as nests and to store honey. You'll dip this honeycomb in chocolate for an even sweeter taste.

INGREDIENTS

170 g granulated sugar
2 tablespoons honey
2 tablespoons water
1½ teaspoons bicarbonate of
   soda
200 g bar of plain chocolate

EQUIPMENT

baking tray
baking parchment
weighing scales
medium saucepan
measuring and mixing spoons
jam thermometer
whisk or wooden spoon
microwave-safe bowl

1 Line the baking tray with baking parchment. Spray with cooking spray.

2 In a medium saucepan, combine the sugar, honey and water. Stir only enough to moisten the sugar. Attach a jam thermometer to the saucepan.

3 Cook over medium-high heat, without stirring. As the sugar melts, small bubbles will form, then larger bubbles. The sugar will begin to caramelise, turning golden brown. Heat to 150°C, for about 5 to 10 minutes. Do not stir. Remove the pan from the heat.

4 Quickly whisk the bicarbonate of soda into the hot syrup. The syrup will foam up. Stir only enough to mix the ingredients, about 5 seconds.

5 Immediately pour the mixture onto the baking tray. Don't spread out the mixture, or the bubbles will pop. Allow the honeycomb mixture to cool until firm, about 1 hour. Break the honeycomb into pieces.

6 Melt the chocolate in the microwave or in a heatproof bowl over simmering water. Dip half of each piece of honeycomb into the melted chocolate. Allow to cool. Store in an airtight container in a cool, dry place.

TIP..

Sugar is hygroscopic. That means it attracts water. Honeycomb is mainly sugar. It will absorb moisture from the air. This can turn hard sweets soft. If you live in a humid place, it is best to eat the honeycomb within a day or two. In a dry climate, it may last up to two weeks if properly stored.

Kitchen Science

BUBBLY BICARB

Bicarbonate of soda is a type of salt. When heated above 79°C (175°F), it creates a gas. This gas is carbon dioxide. The gas makes bubbles that help baked foods, such as cupcakes, rise. The same thing happens when the honeycomb mixture is heated. The carbon dioxide creates bubbles. It's important not to stir the mixture too much after adding the bicarbonate of soda. This allows the air bubbles to stay large, creating the crispy honeycomb treat.

Lemonade ice lollies with berry skewers

Lemonade is tangy and sweet. It's the perfect drink for a hot day. What could be better than that? Lemonade ice lollies! Yoghurt makes these cool treats creamy. Rainbow sprinkles add fun colours. Skewered berries provide a tasty surprise. But you don't have to wait for a heatwave. Try this treat any time!

INGREDIENTS

150 g fresh raspberries
150 g fresh blackberries
440 ml plain full-fat yoghurt
2 tablespoons milk
60 ml lemon juice
2 tablespoons honey
45 g rainbow sprinkles

EQUIPMENT

6 ice-lolly sticks
weighing scales
blender or mixing bowl
    and spoon
6 large ice-lolly moulds

1 Skewer two to four berries on each ice-lolly stick. Push the stick through the middle of the berry. Alternate raspberries and blackberries. Set aside.

2 Mix the yoghurt, milk, lemon juice and honey in a blender or by hand. Blend until smooth. Taste a bit and add more lemon juice or honey if you wish.

3 Gently stir in the rainbow sprinkles. Pour the mixture into the ice-lolly moulds, filling each about halfway.

4 Gently insert the skewered ice-lolly sticks into the moulds. Top off the lollies with more of the yoghurt mixture. The lollies will expand slightly as they freeze, so do not overfill.

5 Freeze until hard, for at least 6 hours. To remove the lollies from their moulds, run them under warm water for 10 to 15 seconds.

Kitchen Science

FREEZING OR MELTING?

Every liquid has a temperature at which it typically turns into a solid. This is known as a freezing point. Water freezes at 0 degrees Celsius (°C) or 32 degrees Fahrenheit (°F). The freezing point for a liquid is usually the same as the melting point for the solid version of the same substance. In other words, ice (a solid) has a melting point of 0°C, when it becomes water. Water (a liquid) has a freezing point of 0°C, when it becomes ice. Other substances have different freezing points. Milk freezes at slightly below 0°C. Yoghurt freezes at an even lower temperature.

Malted ice cream

Malted milk powder gives chocolate ice cream a toasted caramel flavour. Malt powder contains several ingredients, but the grain barley is what gives it its flavour. Taste this ice cream and discover a great new flavour to add to your list of favourites!

TIP ·

Try your homemade ice cream in a milkshake! Blend 240ml of the softened ice cream with 60ml of milk for each shake.

INGREDIENTS

75 g plain chocolate (85% cocoa solids)
150 g caster sugar
75 g malted drink powder
40 g cocoa powder
480 ml whole milk
120 ml double pouring cream
2 eggs
1 tablespoon vanilla extract
¼ teaspoon salt
whipped cream and cherries, optional

EQUIPMENT

weighing scales
knife or food processor
medium saucepan
whisk
medium bowl
measuring spoons
large storage container
ice cream maker, or chilled cake tin
    and electric mixer or blender

1 Finely chop the chocolate with a knife or in a food processor.

2 In a saucepan, mix the sugar, malted drink powder, cocoa powder and chopped chocolate. Whisk in the milk and cream. Cook over medium heat, stirring often, until the mixture is smooth and combined. Remove from heat.

3 Break the eggs into a medium bowl and whisk them. Very slowly pour a small amount of the hot mixture into the eggs, whisking continuously. Make sure it is well blended. Then slowly pour the egg mixture back into the saucepan with the rest of the milk mixture. Make sure you add the mixture slowly so the eggs don't cook. Stir continuously as you combine.

4 Cook on a very low heat, stirring constantly, for about 2 minutes. The mixture should thicken enough to leave a coating on the back of a spoon.

5 Remove the saucepan from the heat. Whisk in the vanilla extract and salt.

6 Pour the mixture into a storage container and seal it. Refrigerate for at least 2 hours, up to overnight.

7 Pour the mixture into the canister of an ice cream maker. Freeze according to manufacturer's instructions. If you don't have an ice cream maker, pour the mixture into a cake tin that's been chilled in the freezer. Freeze for 45 minutes. Take out and blend with an electric mixer or blender. Return to the freezer and repeat every 30 minutes for 2 to 3 hours until frozen.

8 Serve in a bowl and top with whipped cream and cherries if you'd like.

Kitchen Science

WATER VERSUS ICE

Water is made up of molecules. These are the smallest part of a substance. They are too small to see without a microscope. As a liquid, water molecules move around each other. But when water freezes into ice, the water molecules arrange into structures called ice crystals. The lower the temperature, the more quickly water freezes. The ice crystals stay small. When temperatures are closer to freezing (0°C or 32°F), water turns to ice more slowly. The ice crystals are larger. Large ice crystals can affect a food's texture, making it grainy. An ice cream maker prevents large ice crystals from forming by churning (mixing) the liquid ingredients as they freeze. That's also why you need to take the ice cream out of the freezer and stir if you're not using an ice cream maker. Stirring helps keep large ice crystals from forming.

Chocolate mousse in chocolate cups

Some serving plates and bowls make food look pretty, but they're usually forgotten when the meal is over. But no one will forget these bowls made out of chocolate! They're filled with fluffy, frozen chocolate mousse and decorated with chocolate shavings.

INGREDIENTS

150 g chocolate chips
15 g butter
225 g caster sugar
150 g cocoa powder
720 ml whipping cream
2 teaspoons vanilla extract
chocolate shavings to decorate

EQUIPMENT

8-cup cupcake tin and cases
cooking spray
weighing scales
microwave-safe bowl
pastry brush
mixing bowl
measuring spoons
electric mixer

1 Place eight cupcake cases in the cupcake tin. Spray them with cooking spray.

2 Place the chocolate chips and butter in a microwave-safe bowl. Heat it on medium high for 1 minute. Then stir. Heat for additional 30-second intervals as necessary, until the chocolate is smooth.

3 Divide the chocolate among the eight cupcake cases. Using a pastry brush, brush the chocolate evenly on the inside of each cupcake case.

4 Chill the chocolate cups in the fridge until hardened, for at least 30 minutes.

5 Make the chocolate mousse. In a mixing bowl, combine the sugar and cocoa. Blend in the cream and vanilla extract. Beat with an electric mixer until the mixture forms soft peaks.

6 Remove the chocolate cups from the fridge. Check for any holes. Patch them with a dollop of melted chocolate. Peel off the cases and discard. Put the chocolate cups back into the cupcake tin. Divide the chocolate mousse among the chocolate cups. Freeze for at least 2 hours.

7 Decorate the chocolate mousse with chocolate shavings. Serve immediately.

TIP

This recipe asks you to mix until soft peaks form. To test your peaks, stop the mixer and lift the beater. The mix is ready when the beater leaves a peak or point in the mixture, and the top of the peak curls down.

Handy hints

Get great results every time by following some basic steps.

BAKING TIPS

• Use unsalted butter unless the recipe says otherwise. Butter and eggs should be at room temperature. Take them out of the fridge at least 30 minutes before you start baking.

• When baking cookies, put an oven rack on the middle shelf of the oven. Then turn on your oven and let it fully preheat. These steps help ensure the cookies bake evenly.

• To grease a baking tray, rub a very thin layer of butter on the tray with a piece of kitchen roll.

• Use a spoon to scoop flour onto your scales when weighing it out. This helps to make sure you measure accurately.

• Measure ingredients carefully. For teaspoon and tablespoon measurements, use specific measuring spoons. Fill the spoons with the ingredient level across the top, not piled up (unless the recipe calls for 'heaped' spoonfuls).

• To get orange or lemon zest, use a fine grater. Shave slivers of the darkest outside part of the peel only and avoid the pith (the white bit under the peel).

• Set a timer for the lowest time mentioned in the recipe. When the timer dings, check your cookies or cakes to make sure they don't burn.

PROPER MIXING

You may see several mixing terms, with slight differences in meaning:

• **beat** mix ingredients well and add in air, either with a mixer or with a spoon, using an up-and-down and circular motion; beating until something is frothy means it is foamy and has tiny air bubbles

• **blend** mix ingredients until they are well combined and smooth

• **cream** mix sugar and a fat such as butter until smooth, light and creamy

• **fold** gently mix ingredients. Folding is used when the mixture has a lot of air that you don't want to release. Run your spoon or spatula along the side of the mixture, across the bottom of the bowl, and back up. This brings some of the mixture from the bottom up to the top.

• **whisk** make a mixture light and fluffy by beating vigorously

Glossary

caramelise cook sugar until it turns brown

carbon dioxide colourless, odourless gas in the air that people and animals breathe out; some chemicals react with heat to make carbon dioxide

energy ability to do work; energy exists in several forms, including heat

freezing point temperature at which a liquid turns into a solid

heat transfer of energy from one object to another

hygroscopic easily absorbing moisture from the air

melting point temperature at which a solid will turn into a liquid

mixture combination of two or more substances that are mixed together but not chemically combined together

molecule smallest particle of a substance that retains all the properties of that substance

radiation tiny particles sent out from radioactive material

syrup thick, sweet liquid made by dissolving sugar in water

temperature degree of hotness or coldness of something

Find out more

Books

Children's Book of Baking (Usborne Cookbooks), Fiona Patchett (Usborne, 2009)

Complete Children's Cookbook, DK (DK Children, 2015)

The Kew Gardens Children's Cookbook: Plant, Cook, Eat! Caroline Craig and Joe Archer (Wayland, 2016)

Websites

www.bbcgoodfood.com/recipes/collection/kids-cooking
Find more great recipes to try!

www.dkfindout.com/uk/science/solids-liquids-and-gases/ reversible-and-irreversible-changes
Find out more about the chemical changes that happen to foods as they cook.